Fact Attack

The Byte-Sized World of Technology!

by Melvin and Gilda Berger
illustrations by Frank Rocco
& Sarah Watanabe-Rocco

Scholastic Inc.

Photos ©: cover top right: Andrey Armyagov/Shutterstock; cover center: Blend Images/Shutterstock; cover bottom left: Bloomberg/Getty Images; back cover train: View Stock/Thinkstock; 1 and throughout: Ed Miller/Scholastic Inc.; 3: picturedesigner/Thinkstock; 4: Evgeny Moerman/Dreamstime; 5 left: © Stevo Rood; 5 right: Dragoneye/Dreamstime; 6 bottom: belterz/iStockphoto; 7 top: gvm61/Thinkstock; 7 bottom: mphillips007/iStockphoto; 8 stone tools: Sergio Bertino/Dreamstime; 8 using fire: denisgo/Thinkstock; 8 bows and arrows: Egmont Strigl/imagebr/age fotostock; 8 farming: Elena Elisseeva/Dreamstime; 8 bricks: Dreamstime.com Agency/Dreamstime; 9 weaving: Sophie-james/Dreamstime; 9 balance scale: Perseomedusa/Dreamstime; 9 wheels: jgroup/Thinkstock; 9 sailing ships: Empire331/Dreamstime; 9 writing: Photos.com/Thinkstock; 9 glass: Adam Woolfitt/robertharding/Newscom; 9 alphabet: mr-moda/Thinkstock; 10-11: Typhoonski/Dreamstime; 12: Xinhua News Agency/Getty Images; 13 center: Culture Club/Getty Images; 13 bottom: Bert Folsom/Dreamstime; 14 center: Ye group and Baxley/JILA/NIST; 14 bottom: NASA; 15 center: Eyematrix/Thinkstock; 15 bottom: Brooklyn Museum of Art, New York, USA/Bridgeman Images; 16-17: Imaginechina/AP Images; 18 top: dreamnikon/Thinkstock; 18 center: Courtesy of Foldscope; 19: SuperStock/Getty Images; 20: Justin Sullivan/Getty Images; 21 center: Il Capitolo dei Domenicani/Wikipedia; 21 bottom: Tesla/UPI/Newscom; 22-23 background: Auris/iStockphoto; 22-23 shelves: fischerscoop/Thinkstock; 22 printing press: Josse Christophel/Alamy Images; 22 telescope: Science & Society Picture Library/Getty Images; 22 steam train: Science Museum/Wikipedia; 22 steamboat: From The New York Public Library; 22 electric motor: Royal Institution of Great Britain/Science Source; 22 refrigerator: Science & Society Picture Library/Getty Images; 22 telephone: George Rinhart/Getty Images; 22 lightbulb: Science & Society Picture Library/Getty Images; 22 radio: Science & Society Picture Library/Getty Images; 22 airplane: Library of Congress; 22 television: Bettmann/Getty Images; 22 rocket engine: NASA; 23 computer: Bettmann/Getty Images; 23 robot: Critical Past LLC; 23 laser: Bettmann/Getty Images; 23 video game: Kris Connor/Getty Images; 23 VCR: Mangos/Wikipedia; 23 internet: Fred Prouser/Reuters; 23 cell phone: Eric Risberg/AP Images; 23 personal computer: Courtesy of the Computer History Museum; 23 mobile computer: Future Publishing/Getty Images; 23 world wide web: FABRICE COFFRINI/Getty Images; 23 smartphone: CARL COURT/Getty Images; 23 DVD: Gonzalomedin/Dreamstime; 23 YouTube: Piero Cruciatti/Dreamstime; 23 iPad: Manaemedia/Dreamstime; 24 center: Science & Society Picture Library/Getty Images; 24 bottom: Science & Society Picture Library/Getty Images; 25 top: View Stock/Thinkstock; 25 center: NASA; 25 bottom: Bettmann/Getty Images; 26-27: VCG/Getty Images; 28: Tomas1111/Dreamstime; 29 center: photo360/Dreamstime; 29 bottom: NASA; 30 top: Helena Bilková/Dreamstime; 30 center: USPTO; 30 bottom: Library of Congress; 31 top: Bettmann/Getty Images; 31 center left: Bettmann/Getty Images; 31 center right: Division of Work & Industry, National Museum of American History, Smithsonian Institution; 31 bottom: Jsingh1699/Dreamstime; 32: Corbis/Getty Images; 33 center: Afxhome/Dreamstime; 33 bottom: Jim Pringle/AP Images; 34: Bettmann/Getty Images; 35 top: STAN HONDA/Getty Images; 35 bottom: 350jb/Dreamstime; 36-37 background: stockchairatgfx/Thinkstock; 37: Bloomberg/Getty Images; 38 top: R. Gino Santa Maria/Shutterfree, Llc/Dreamstime; 38 bottom: Parkpoom/Thinkstock; 39 top: INTERFOTO/Alamy Images; 40: Library of Congress; 41 center: bonniej/iStockphoto; 41 bottom: DISNEY/PIXAR/Rona/age fotostock; 42 center left: genekrebs/Thinkstock; 42 center right: USPTO; 42 bottom: FOR ALAN/Alamy Images; 43 top left: Fox Photos/Getty Images; 43 top right: FOR ALAN/Alamy Images; 43 center & bottom left: Nationaal Archief/Collectie Spaarnestad/Het Leven/Fotograaf onbekend; 43 bottom right: USPTO; 44: Jaroslaw Kilian/Dreamstime; 45 top: Thierry Falise/Getty Images; 45 bottom: Bobnevv/Shutterstock; 48: Culture Club/Getty Images; 49 top: Library of Congress; 49 bottom: Baltimore Sun/Getty Images; 50-51 background: Indiansummer/Dreamstime; 52: Rainer Pauschert/Dreamstime; 53 center: Jan Kovalcik/Dreamstime; 53 bottom: VanderWolfImages/Dreamstime; 55 top: Popartic/iStockphoto; 55 center: Dziurek/Dreamstime; 56-57: Library of Congress; 58: valentinrussanov/Getty Images; 60 top: Ken Faught/Getty Images; 60 center: Sean Gallup/Getty Images; 61: Andreas Weber/Dreamstime; 62 top left: Georgiy Pashin/Thinkstock; 62 top center: Photick/Frederic Cirou/Thinkstock; 62 top right: USPTO; 62 center left: The National Archives and Records Administration; 62 center right: ricardoreitmeyer/iStockphoto; 62 bottom left: Museum of Ingenuity J. Armand Bombardier; 62 bottom right: Pahham/Dreamstime; 63 top left: USPTO; 63 top center: Courtesy of Jon Fleck; 63 top right: USPTO; 63 center left: KK Greer/Wristies; 63 center right: KRT/Newscom; 63 bottom left: Courtesy of By Kids For Kids, Co.; 63 bottom center: Courtesy Michael Heater; 63 bottom right: Mark Tucker; 64 top: ilbusca/iStockphoto; 64 bottom: Photo 12/Alamy Images; 65 center: Jumpeestudio/Thinkstock; 66-67: xavdlp/Thinkstock; 69: The Asahi Shimbun/Getty Images; 70 top: Science & Society Picture Library/Getty Images; 70 bottom: Tim C Cox/The Bristol Herald-Courier via AP Images; 71: Gil.K/Shutterstock; 72 top: Evans/Getty Images; 72 bottom: NASA; 73: Bettmann/Getty Images; 76-77 background: Oleg Golovnev/Shutterstock; 76 top left: Xavier ROSSI/Getty Images; 76 top right: Mikhail Blajenov/Dreamstime; 76 bottom left: Viktor Gladkov/Dreamstime; 76 bottom right: DrMadra/Shutterstock; 76 top & center sketches: Janaka Dharmasena/Shutterstock; 76 bottom sketch: Janaka Dharmasena/Shutterstock; 77 steam engine: Museo Nazionale della Scienza e della Tecnologia 'Leonardo Da Vinci', Milan, Italy/Photo © Tarker/Bridgeman Images; 77 airplane: leoblanchette/Thinkstock; 77 bicycle: Liudmila Shchaeva/Dreamstime; 77 telescope: Biblioteca Ambrosiana, Milan, Italy/De Agostini Picture Library/Metis e Mida Informatica/Veneranda Biblioteca Ambrosiana/Bridgeman Images; 77 helicopter: H3c7or/Thinkstock; 77 swimming shoes: David Honl/ZUMA Press/Newscom; 77 eyeglasses: RMN-Grand Palais/Art Resource, NY; 77 top sketch: Janaka Dharmasena/Shutterstock; 77 left sketch: JanakaMaharageDharmasena/Thinkstock; 77 bottom sketch: JanakaMaharageDharmasena/Thinkstock; 78 top: Jamalludin Bin Abu Seman Din/Dreamstime; 78 bottom: Stocktrek Images/Thinkstock; 79 center: JaysonPhotography/Thinkstock; 79 bottom: USAF/Getty Images; 80: Bettmann/Getty Images; 81: Atlantik-Solar Project, Autonomous Systems Lab, ETH Zurich; 82-83 background: noppadon_sangpeam/Thinkstock; 82 top left: Private Collection/© Look and Learn/Bridgeman Images; 82 top right: Sean Pavone/Dreamstime; 82 center left: Taesmileland/Dreamstime; 82 center right: Print Collector/Getty Images; 82 bottom left: George Rinhart/Getty Images; 82 bottom right: Science & Society Picture Library/Getty Images; 83 upper top right: Satirus/Thinkstock; 83 top left: davidtidwell86/Thinkstock; 83 top right: TOM COPELAND/AP/REX/Shutterstock; 83 center left: Bettmann/Getty Images; 83 center right: Mandrixta/Thinkstock; 83 bottom left: Josep Curto/123RF; 83 bottom right: atilayunal/iStockphoto; 84: The Yomiuri Shimbun/AP Images; 85 top: ESA/ATG medialab; 85 bottom: bedo/Thinkstock; 86: NASA; 87 top: VCG/Getty Images; 87 bottom: Mosaymay/Dreamstime; 88 patent: Wikipedia; 88 paper: Liz Van Steenburgh/Dreamstime; 88 soap: DNY59/iStockphoto; 89 top: Malekas85/Thinkstock; 89 plane: Karpiyon/Thinkstock; 89 center: Huguette Roe/Dreamstime; 89 bottom: NASA; 92-93 GT: SWNS/Splash News/Newscom; 92-93 GT background: Archana Bhartia/Dreamstime; 92-93 Spirit: KEYSTONE PICTURES USA/age fotostock; 92-93 Spirit background: Sallyeva/Dreamstime; 92-93 Maglev: YMZK-Photo/Shutterstock; 92-93 Ack: Courtesy ACK Technologies Inc.; 92-93 Ack background: Thomas Croonen/Dreamstime; 92-93 Thrust: Dusan Vranic/AP Images; 92-93 Thrust background: Jill Lang/Dreamstime; 92-93 Blackbird: Dan Simonsen/Shutterstock; 92-93 Blackbird background: Rangizzz/Dreamstime; 92-93 Horizons: Orlando Sentinel/Getty Images; 92-93 Horizons background: Dmitriy Karelin/Dreamstime; 93 flag: Maksym Yemelyanov/Dreamstime.

Library of Congress Cataloging-in-Publication Data available

ISBN 978-1-338-04186-6

10 9 8 7 6 5 4 3 2 1 17 18 19 20 21

Printed in the U.S.A. 40
First edition, September 2017

Book design by Sunny Lee & Marissa Asuncion
Photo Research by Cian O'Day

Did you know that the **V2 rocket** was the world's first man-made object in outer space?

Or that Americans check their **smartphones** an average of 46 times a day?

Inside **THIS BOOK** are 372 more

WACKY, CRAZY, WILD, UNBELIEVABLE, SILLY, AWESOME

facts about technology that will AMAZE you!

Turn the page and let your FACTASTIC adventure begin!

#1

Before the invention of modern **toothbrushes**, people used tree twigs to clean their teeth.

#2

Skyscrapers are built to sway and shake without falling down.

#3

Some **pioneers** attached sails to their covered wagons to go faster.

#4

Five thousand years ago, people made **ice skates** out of animal bones.

#5

The world's tallest **bicycle** is taller than an elephant.

I found the battery!
That's a piece of hair.

#6

The smallest **battery** is thinner than a strand of hair.

#7

One ounce of **gold** can be stretched to make a wire 50 miles long!

#8

There are only two sets of **escalators** in the state of Wyoming.

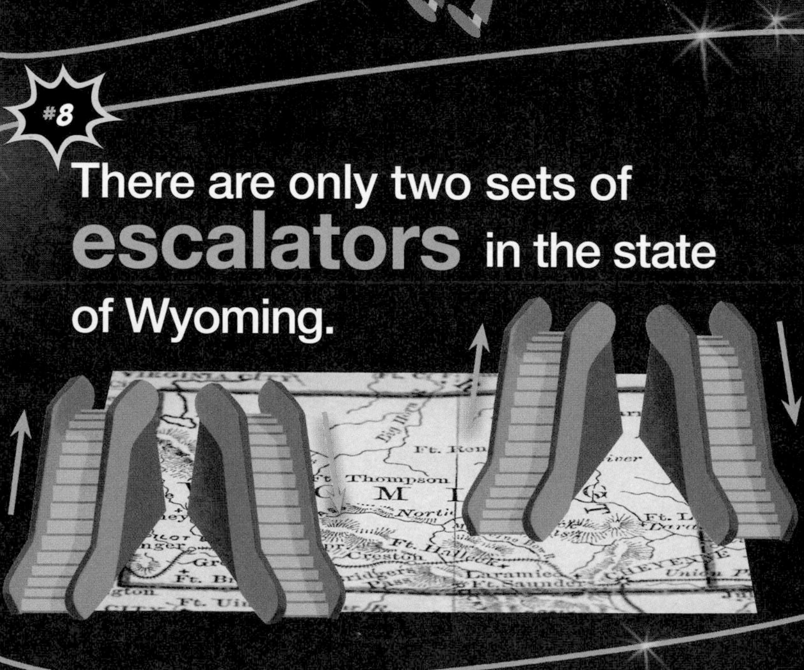

#9

A nuclear submarine

can stay underwater for about three months before coming up for supplies.

#10

May 20, 1873, is the "birthday" of **blue jeans**.

#11

Levi Strauss and Jacob Davis used metal rivets on pants' pockets for the first time, so they would not tear.

#12

Some of the world's most important **inventions** and advances in **technology** date back to the Stone Age.*

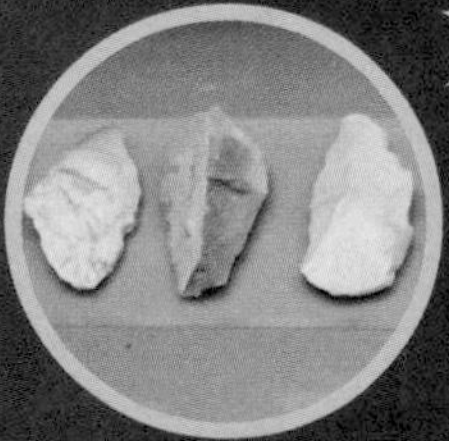

#13

Stone tools

2.6 million BCE**

#14

Using fire

1.2 million BCE

#15

Bows and arrows

69,000 BCE

#16

Farming

13,000 BCE

#17

Bricks

8,000 BCE

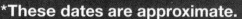

*These dates are approximate.

**BCE stands for "Before Common Era."

#18
Weaving
5,000 BCE

#19
Balance scale
5,000 BCE

#20
Wheels
3,500 BCE

#21
Sailing ships
3,400 BCE

#22
Writing
3,000 BCE

#23
Glass
2,500 BCE

#24
Alphabet
1,800 BCE

#25

Robots in Qatar and the United Arab Emirates ride camels in races.

#26

Wave farms generate electricity from ocean waves.

#27

Doctors who play **video games** make better surgeons.

#28 *They have especially good reaction times and hand-eye coordination.*

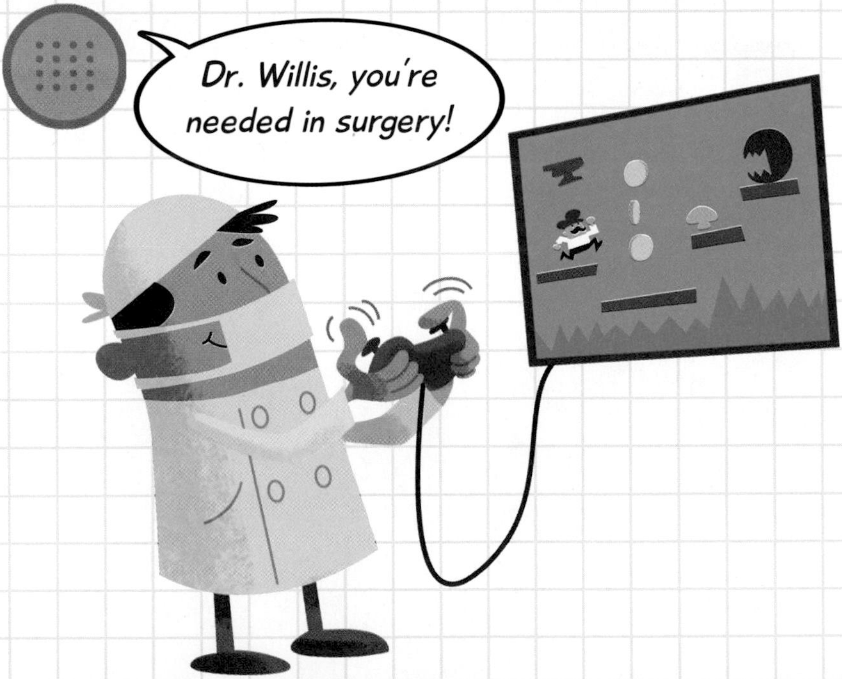
Dr. Willis, you're needed in surgery!

#29

Nomophobia is the fear of being without a **smartphone**.

#30

Yahoo was named for the rude, rough characters in the book *Gulliver's Travels*.

#31

The founders jokingly called each other "yahoos."

#32

In 1849, Walter Hunt twisted a piece of wire and invented the first **safety pin**.

#33

Today's **cell phones** have more powerful computers than those that guided Apollo 11 to the moon.

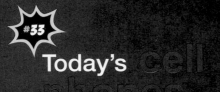

Power's out again. Anyone have a cell phone?

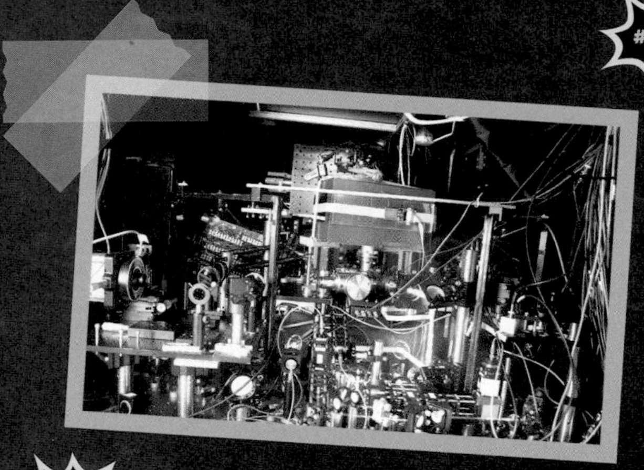

#34

The newest **atomic clock** will not lose or gain a second in 15 billion years.

#35

The **Hubble Space Telescope** was named for Edwin Hubble, a leading 20th-century astronomer.

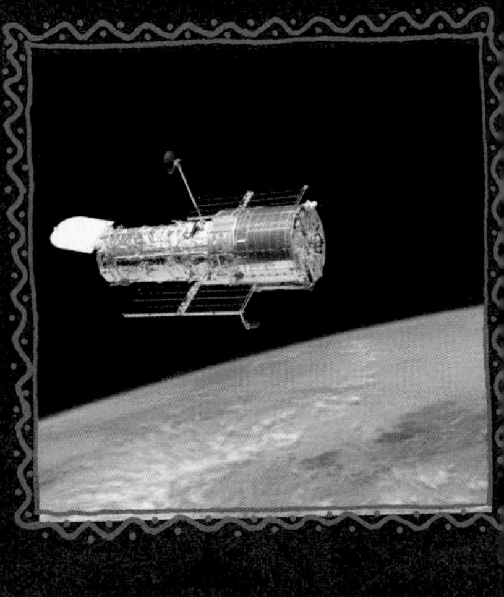

#36

It took more than two years to grind and polish the telescope's giant mirror.

#37

The **cell phone** was invented in 1973 by Martin Cooper.

#38

This early phone was as big as a brick and weighed two pounds.

#39

Solar, wind, and water **energy** provide 22 percent of the world's needs.

#40

In 1895, the world's first **escalator** was installed at Coney Island, in Brooklyn, New York.

#41

In 2015, 300 teams from 47 countries around the world competed in RoboCup soccer.

#42

The games are fun to watch and also teach people about robots.

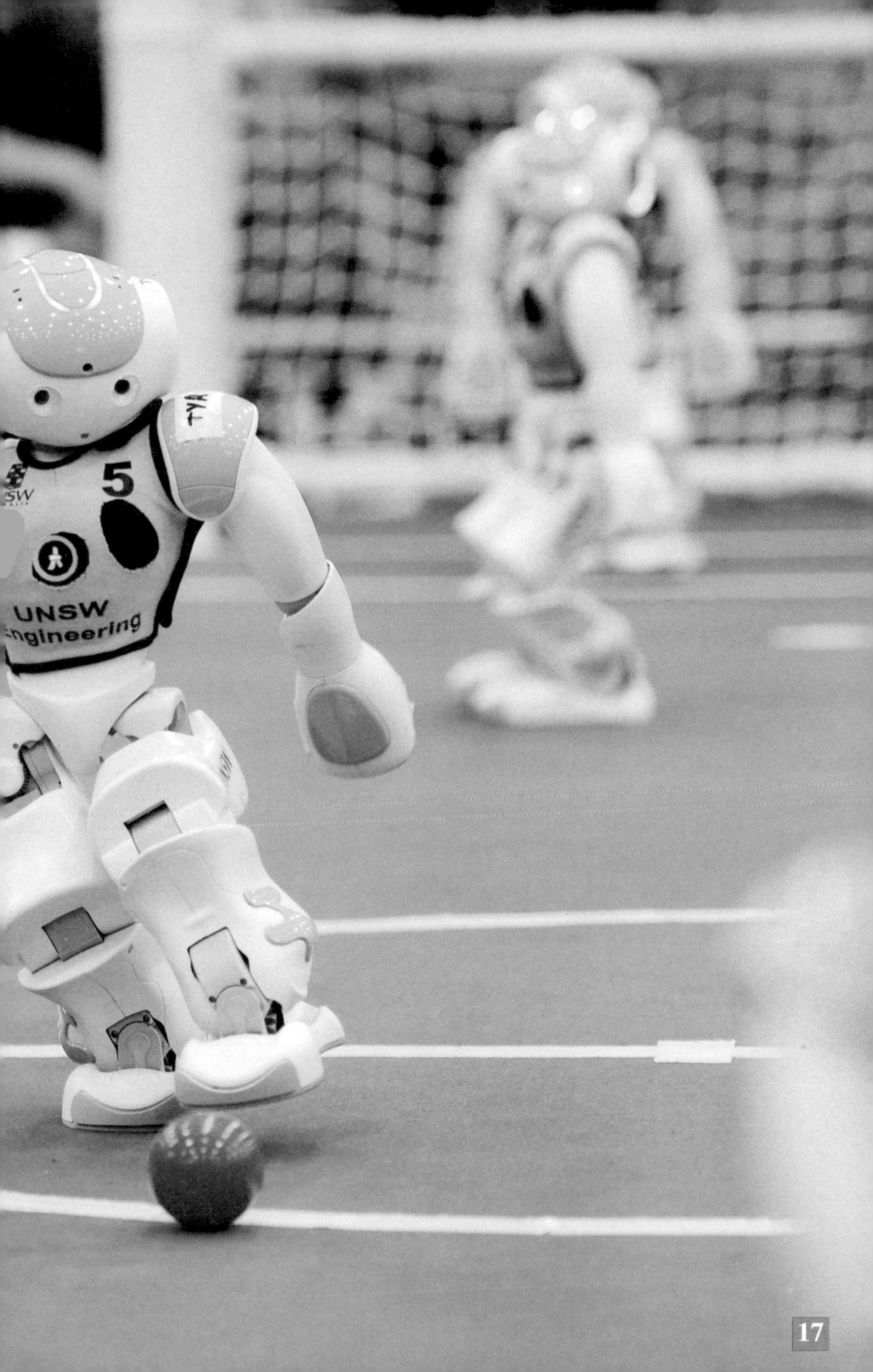
TYA
5
UNSW
Engineering

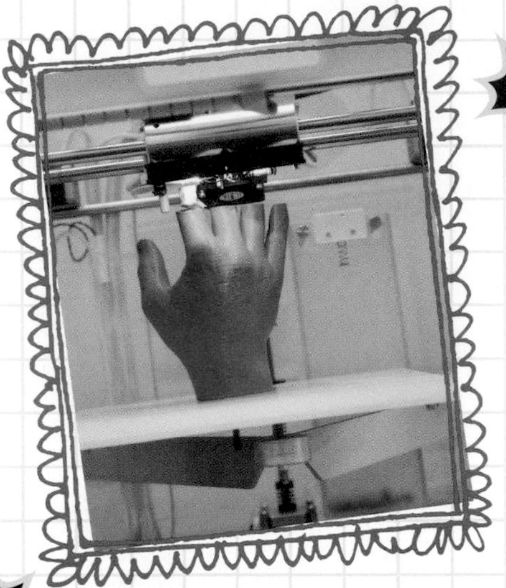

#43

3-D printers

build real objects with layers of plastic or other materials.

#44

The Foldscope microscope

is made of paper with a tiny plastic lens.

#45

It costs only 50 cents to make, and it can magnify objects 2,000 times.

I think I'll call my new computer a Mac.

#46

Macintosh computers, or **Macs**, are named for McIntosh apples.

#47

Hershey's Kisses, some say, got their name from the machine that makes little kissing sounds as it produces the candy.

#48

A small submarine, ***Trieste***, went down nearly 7 miles to the deepest part of the ocean.

#49

It stayed down only 20 minutes because of a cracked window.

#50

The first computer **mouse** was made of wood with two metal wheels.

#51

Its name came from the attached cable, which looked like a mouse's tail.

#52

Louis Daguerre took the first **photograph** of a living person in 1838.

#53

The person had to stay still for 10 minutes while Daguerre took the picture.

Hold still—just nine more minutes!
10 1 2 3 4 5 6 7 8 9

#54

Google comes from "googol" (the number 1 followed by 100 zeroes)—a reminder of the many things that Google can do.

#55

The first **eyeglasses**, invented around 1268 in Italy, were worn only by monks and scholars.

#56

Powerwall 2 is a huge, 264-pound battery that stores energy from solar panels or wind turbines.

#57

From the printing press to the iPad, many of the world's **greatest inventions** have come in the last 600 years.*

#58 Printing press
1450

#59 Telescope
1608

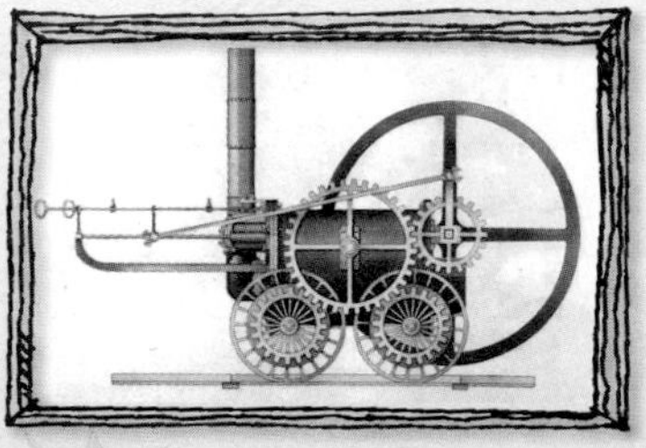

#60 Steam train
1803

#61 Steamboat
1807

#62 Electric motor
1821

#63 Refrigerator
1834

#64 Telephone
1876

#65 Lightbulb
1879

#66 Radio
1895

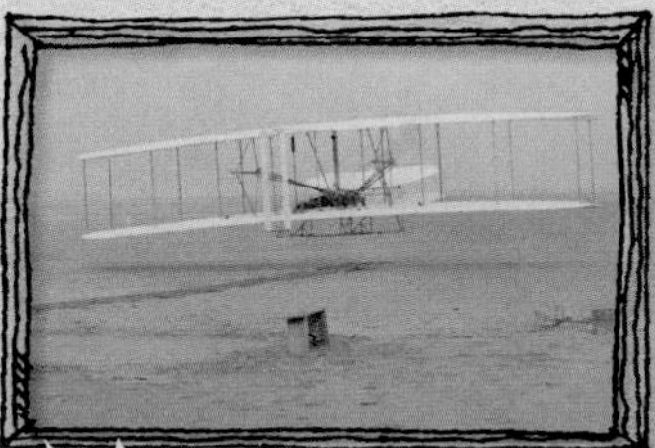

#67 Airplane
1903

#68 Television
1926

#69 Rocket engine
1926

*These dates are approximate.

#70 Computer 1946

#71 Robot 1954

#72 Laser 1960

#73 Video game 1967

#74 Videocassette recorder (VCR) 1969

#75 Internet 1969

#76 Cell phone 1973

#77 Personal computer 1974

#78 Mobile computer 1981

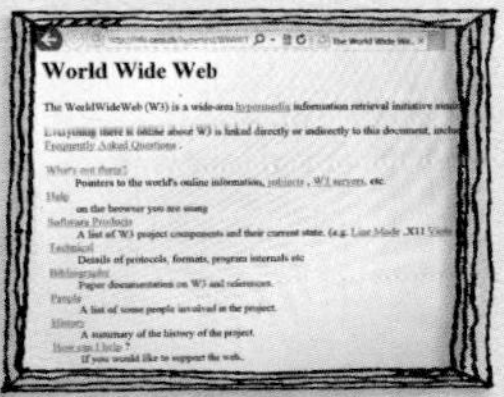

#79 World Wide Web 1991

#80 Smartphone 1992

#81 Digital video disc (DVD) 1995

#82 YouTube 2005

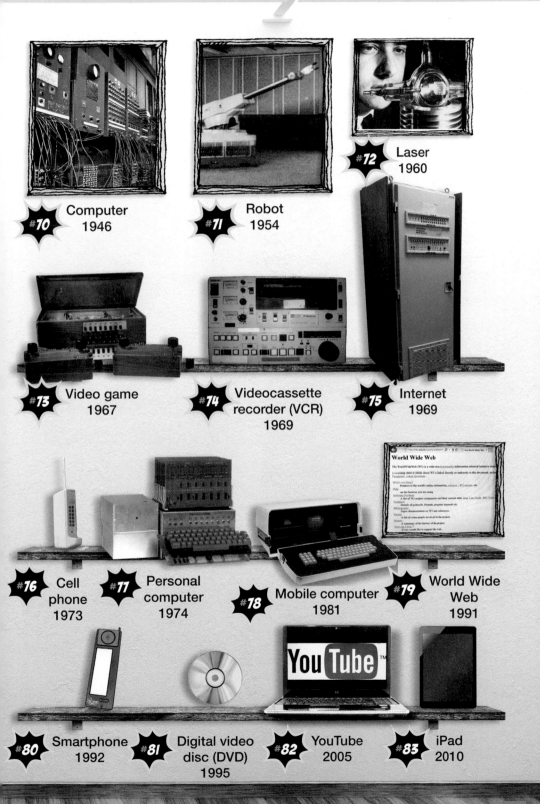

#83 iPad 2010

#84

In 1749, Benjamin Franklin first used the word **battery** for a device that produces a small electric current.

#85

He once used a battery to kill and fry a turkey for some friends.

#86

The first **VCR**—or videocassette recorder—was as big as a piano.

#87

The **fax machine** was invented about 30 years before the telephone.

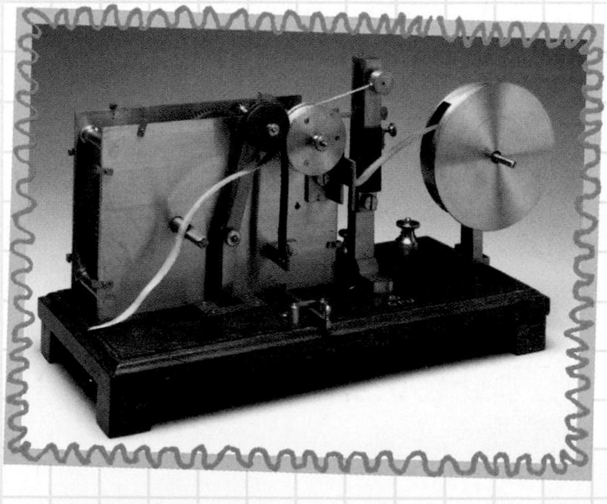

#88

A high-speed **Maglev bullet train** floats above the tracks.

#89 *Maglev stands for "magnetic levitation," since magnets raise and move the train forward.*

#90

In 1957, **Sputnik** was the first artificial satellite to orbit Earth.

#91

Grace Hopper, a computer pioneer, coined the term "**bug**."

#92 *She first used the word when a moth damaged her computer.*

#93

The highest **bridge** in the world is in China.

#94

Its roadway hangs from steel cables attached to towers—more than a third of a mile above the river below.

#95

The world's most powerful computer, the **Sunway TaihuLight**, can do 93 trillion operations a second.

#96

A trillion is 1 followed by 12 zeros.

#97

The top of the **Empire State Building** broadcasts most TV stations for New York City.

#98

The building is struck by lightning about 23 times a year.

#99

X-rays are invisible beams of light that can pass through solid objects.

#100 *People once feared that X-rays would show them naked.*

#101

A modern **jet** can carry more than 400 passengers and fly faster than 600 miles an hour.

#102

An **astronaut's suit** that weighs 280 pounds on Earth is weightless in outer space.

#103

The first cars were built more than a century ago—and they keep getting better and better.

#104

1885
Carl Benz builds the first car.

#105

1894
Alfred Vacheron invents the steering wheel.

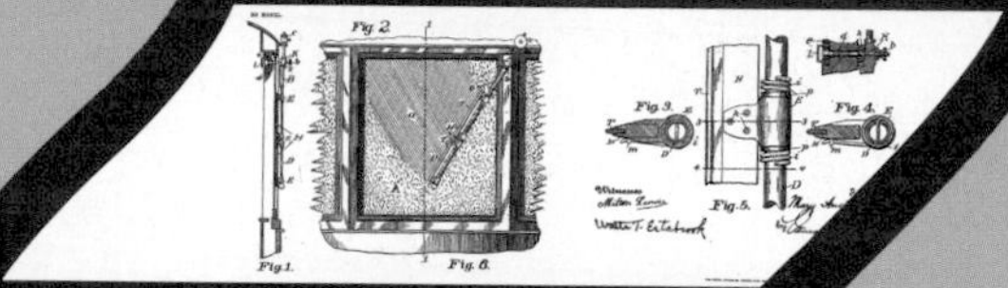

#106

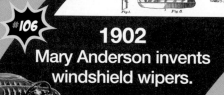

1902
Mary Anderson invents windshield wipers.

#107

1908
Henry Ford builds the first low-priced automobile, the Model T.

#108

1909
Percy Douglas-Hamilton invents turn signals.

#109

1911

Charles Kettering invents the electric, key-operated, self-starter.

#110

1913

Henry Ford invents the assembly line for mass-producing cars.

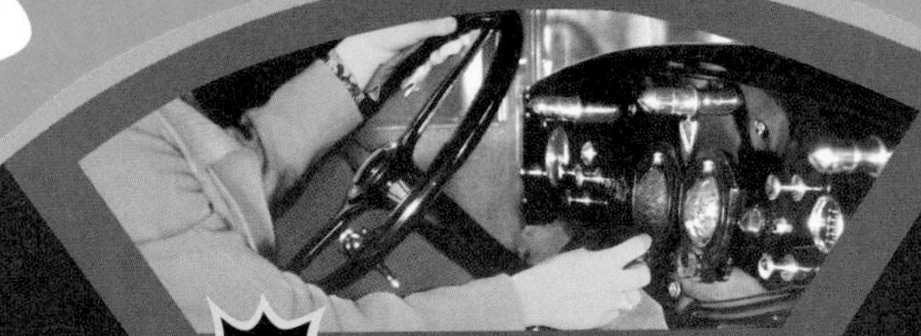

#111

1930

Paul and Joseph Galvin invent the car radio.

#112

1953

John Hetrick and Walter Linderer independently invent the air bag.

#113

1959

Nils Bohlin invents seat belts.

#114

2010

Nissan starts mass-producing all-electric cars.

#115

In 2011, an IBM computer won $1 million playing *Jeopardy!*

$1,000,000
Who's a winner? (THIS GUY!)
$0
This is so unfair!

#116

A fiber-optic cable can carry millions of telephone conversations, TV, and computer signals—all at the same time.

#117

The first fiber-optic cable across the Atlantic Ocean was laid in 1988.

#118

More people have been to the **moon** than to the bottom of the ocean.

#119

Sneakers got their name because wearers could walk around without being heard.

#120

The first live international **television transmission** was on July 23, 1962.

#121

It showed the Statue of Liberty, the Eiffel Tower, and President John F. Kennedy saying a few words.

I can't leave without my peanuts!

#122 Space-mission **engineers** eat peanuts for good luck.

#123 *It started in 1964 as a way of easing their stress before a space shot.*

#124 In 1853, Elisha Otis invented an **elevator** with brakes, which made skyscrapers possible.

#125 *It let people ride to the top floors of tall buildings without fear of crashing down.*

#126

A **computer** beat the world chess champion for the first time in 1996.

#127

A British writer, Sir John Harrington, invented the **flush toilet** around 1596.

#128

He only built two—one for himself and one for Queen Elizabeth I.

#129

A **fiber-optic cable** is made up of very thin threads of glass.

#130

Androids are robots that look and act human.

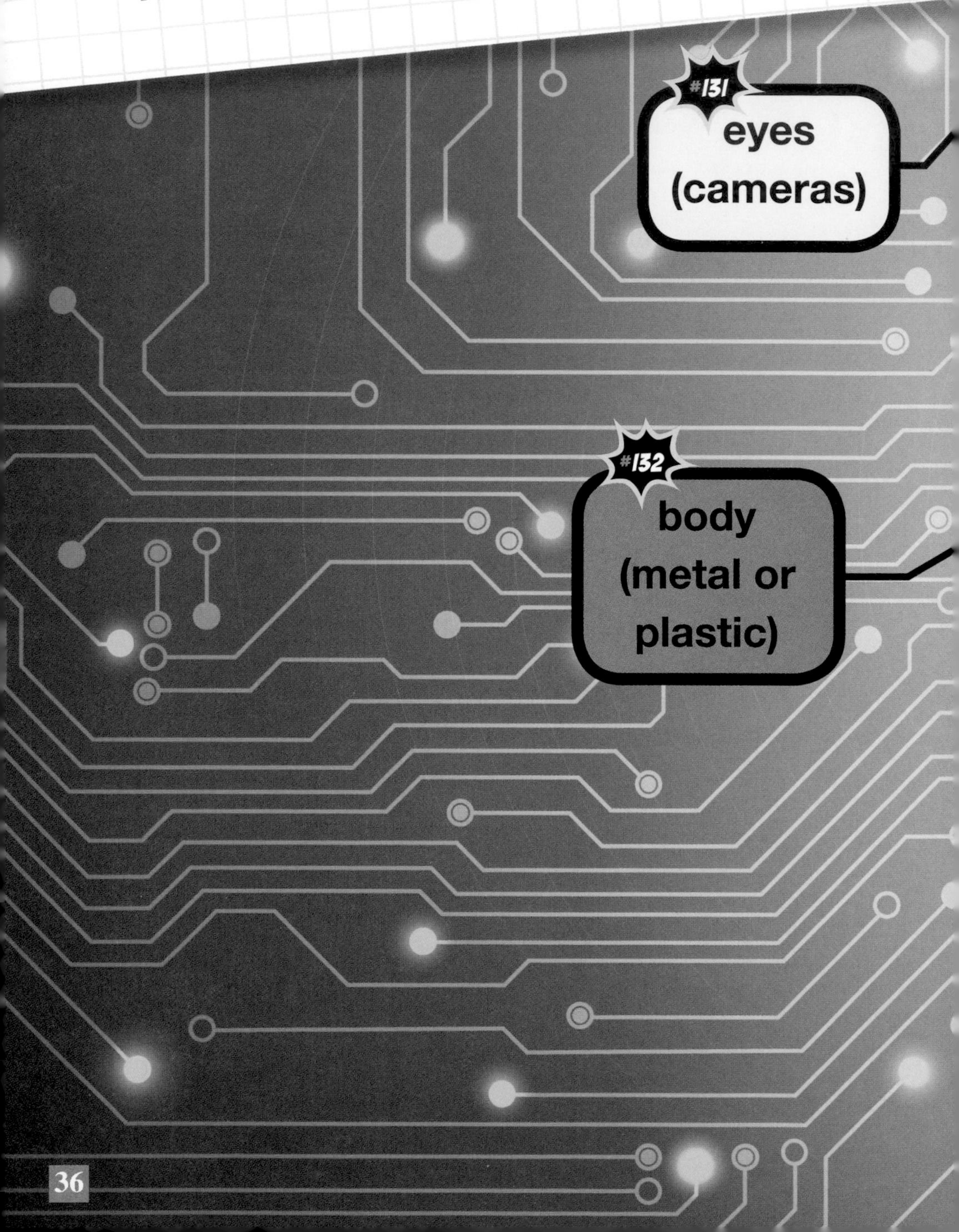

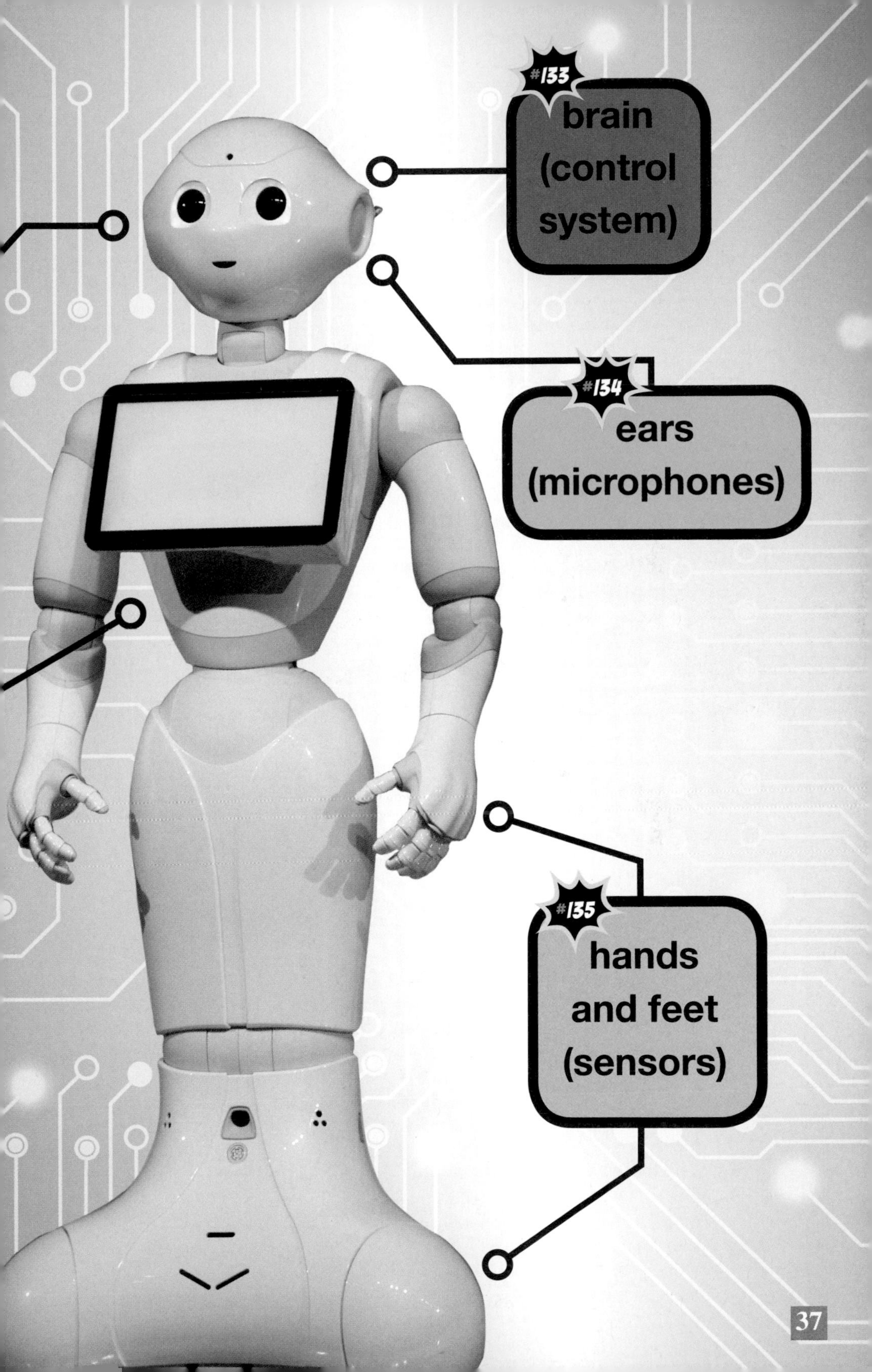
#133
brain (control system)
#134
ears (microphones)
#135
hands and feet (sensors)

#136

Margaret Knight, in 1870, patented her invention of the square-bottom **paper bag** still used for groceries today.

#137

Google answers around three billion questions a day.

#138

The **ballpoint pen** actually has a tiny steel ball in the point.

#139

It was invented by John J. Loud in 1888 as a way to write on leather.

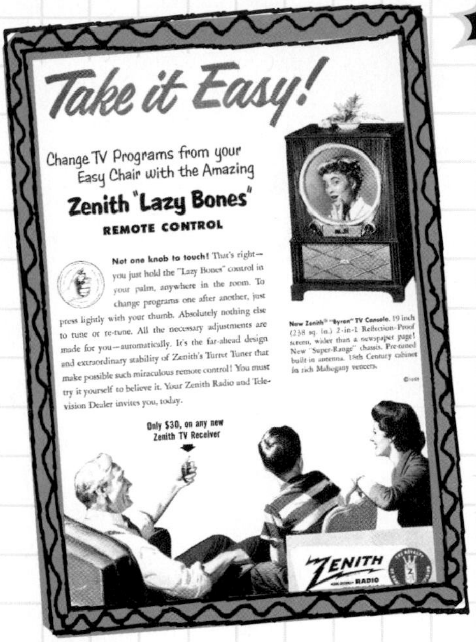

#140

In 1950, "Lazy Bones," the first **TV remote**, was connected by wire to the TV.

#141

Six years later, Robert Adler invented a wireless remote.

#142

Thomas Edison got patents for **1,903 inventions** in the US, and a total of 2,332 worldwide.

#143

His first patent, given on June 1, 1869, was for an electric vote counter.

#144

The first human flight was in a **hot-air balloon** in 1783.

#145

A small fire in an iron basket heated the air in the balloon, so that it rose as high as a 25-story building.

#146

People using computers **blink** about seven times a minute.

#147

Normally, people blink about twenty times a minute.

#148

The first American **alarm clock** was invented by Levi Hutchins in New Hampshire, in 1787.

#149

The problem was it only rang at 4 a.m.—Hutchins's waking time.

#150

Thomas Jennings invented **dry cleaning** in 1821.

#151

Toy Story, released in 1995, was the first computer-animated movie.

#152

The difference between weird and wonderful is sometimes very small.

#153

Some strange-but-true inventions are still waiting to catch on.

#154

Clip-on ice skates, 1837

#155

Parachute hat, 1879

#156

Folding bridge, 1926

#157

One-wheel motorcycle, 1931

#158

Heated police vest, 1932

#159

Ten-wheel all-terrain car, 1936

#160

Mask for snowstorms, 1939

#161

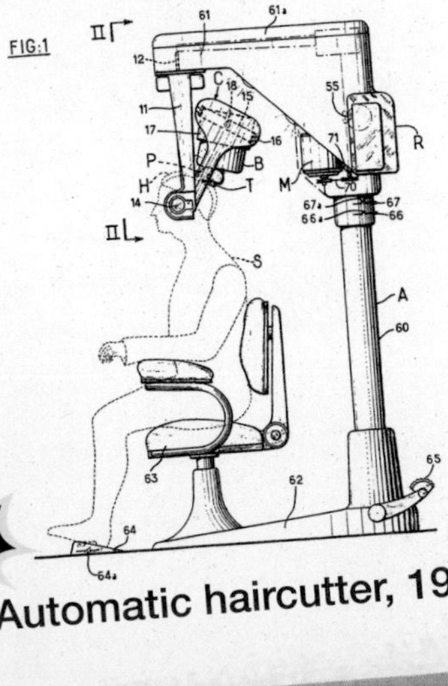

Automatic haircutter, 1966

#162

The ocean liner ***Titanic*** burned up to 825 tons of coal a day on its five-day ill-fated voyage.

#163 *The coal was hand-shoveled into furnaces by 176 men.*

#164

In 1877, Thomas Edison made the world's first **sound recording**.

#165 *He recited "Mary Had a Little Lamb" into the machine—and played back the words.*

#166

The wings of **RoboBees**, one of the smallest drones, beat 120 times a second.

#167

The first bicycles had **NO** pedals.

#168

People moved the bicycles with their feet, like scooters today.

#169

The video game **Tetris** has been downloaded more than 425 million times!

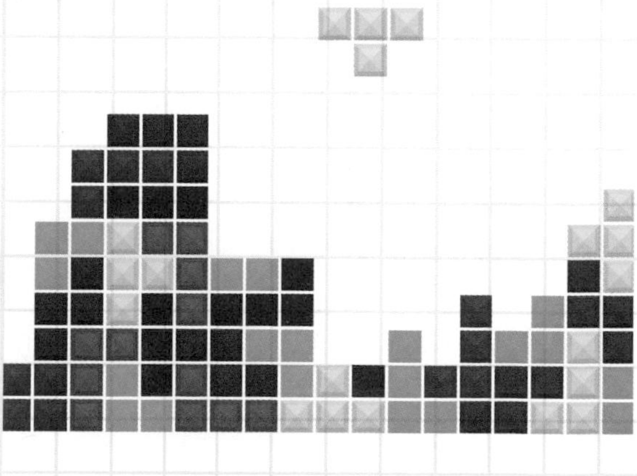

#170

Advances in communication **technology** throughout the years have spread news faster and faster.

#171

It took 5 months to learn that **Christopher Columbus** had discovered America (1492),

#172

2 weeks to learn that **Abraham Lincoln** had been shot (1865),

#173

and 1.3 seconds to learn that **Neil Armstrong** had landed on the moon (1969).

#174

When **radio** was invented it took 38 years to reach 50 million users.

#175

Television took 13 years to reach the same number of people,

#176

the **Internet** took 4 years,

#177

and **Facebook** took only 3 years.

#178

The most ancient tires, around 1300 BCE, were wooden wheels covered in leather.

#179

John Dunlop invented air-filled tires for his son's tricycle in 1888.

#180

In 1894, Guglielmo Marconi, inventor of the **radio**, began his experiments.

#181

Only seven years later, radio messages were being sent across the Atlantic Ocean.

#182

George Washington Carver created more than 300 products from **peanuts**, 118 from sweet potatoes, and 75 from pecans.

#183

After *Toy Story 2* was finished, all copies—except one—were accidentally **erased**.

#184

Student **engineers** used a 3-D printer to make a **bionic arm** for a disabled boy.

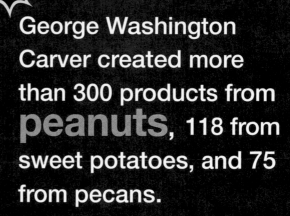

#185

"Bit," "bug," and "cookie" have different meanings for **tech people** than for others.

Check out this list of "techie" words.

WORD	TECHIE MEANING
#186 artificial intelligence (AI)	computers that think like humans
#187 artificial satellite	man-made object that orbits Earth
#188 bit	the smallest amount of data
#189 browser	a program used to move around the Internet
#190 bug	a computer error
#191 byte	eight bits of data
#192 cookie	data saved by a computer

#193 **data**	facts, numbers, or words, especially for computer use
#194 **hack**	to obtain or change computer data illegally
#195 **hardware**	parts of a computer, such as keyboard, monitor, and printer
#196 **network**	a system that connects electronic devices
#197 **operating system (OS)**	software that allows programs to run on a computer
#198 **software**	data or instructions that allow a computer program to run
#199 **techie**	an expert in technology, especially computers
#200 **virus**	a program that damages a computer

#201

A solar furnace in France can melt steel using just the sun's rays.

#202

The GPS, or Global Positioning System, uses about 30 satellites orbiting 12,550 miles above Earth to locate any spot on the planet.

#203

Each satellite sends radio signals to Earth. GPS devices on Earth use signals from at least four satellites to pinpoint an exact location.

Let's find the best donuts on Earth!

#204

"Emoji," which means "pictures" in **Japanese**, started being used in 1999.

#205

The world's most expensive **TV** is made of gold and diamonds and sells for $2,260,000.

#206

Some **driverless cars** do not have a steering wheel, gas pedal, or brake pedal.

#207

They have already covered over one million miles.

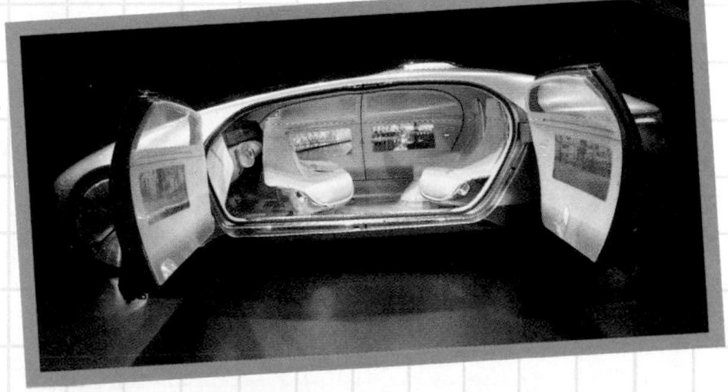

#208

Some astronauts attach **Velcro** inside their helmets to scratch itches.

#209

The **longest bicycle** is more than 117 feet long.

#210 *It has two wheels, like other bicycles, but needs two riders—one to steer and one to pedal.*

#211

Joseph Priestley, famous for his co-discovery of oxygen, called his 1767 invention of **soda**, or sparkling water, his *"happiest"* discovery.

#212

In 1949, Marion Donovan made parents' lives easier by inventing the **disposable diaper.**

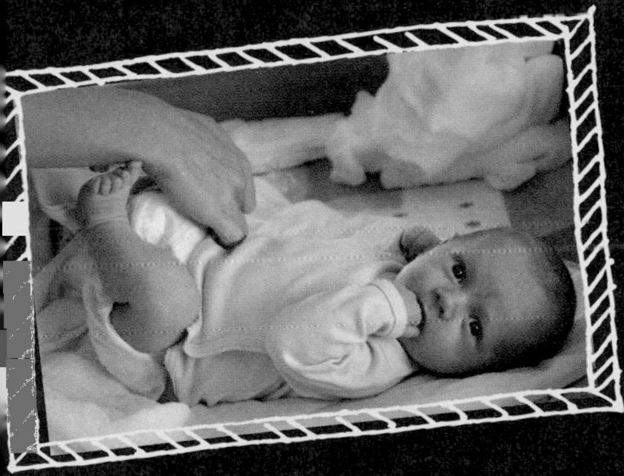

#213

Orville and Wilbur Wright invented the airplane in 1903.

#214

On its first flight, the plane flew about 120 feet—less than half the length of a football field.

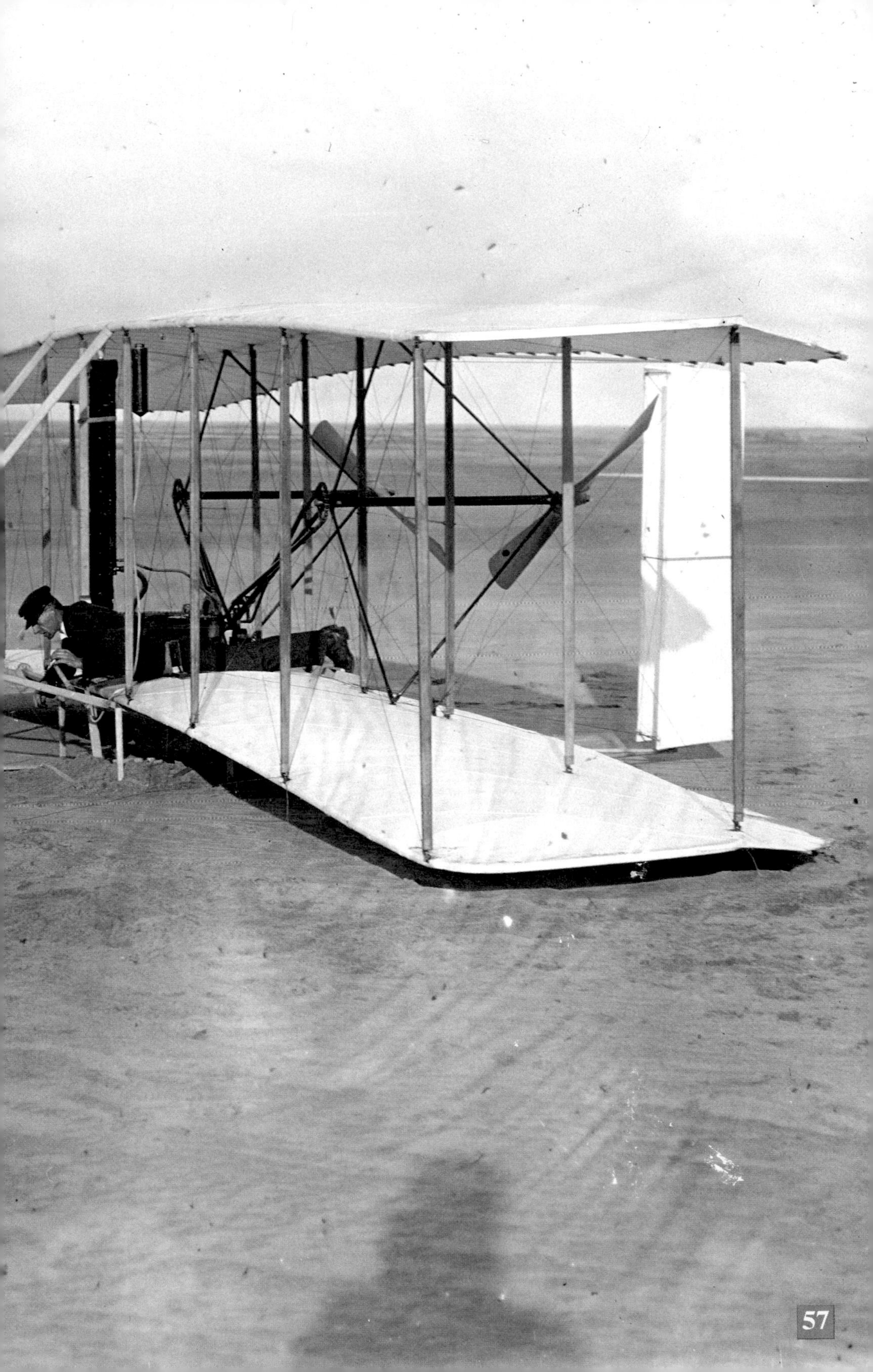

#215

Alexander Graham Bell received a patent for the **telephone** on March 7, 1876.

#216

He was only a few hours ahead of another inventor, Elisha Gray.

#217

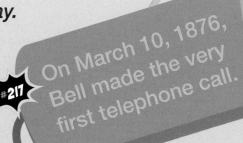

On March 10, 1876, Bell made the very first telephone call.

#218 It was to his assistant in another room.

#219 Bell said, "Watson, come here, I want to see you"—and Watson came!

#220 Alexander Graham Bell wanted the standard greeting to be "Ahoy," but Thomas Edison preferred "Hello."

#221

The longest car has 26 wheels and is 100 feet long.

#222 *It has a king-size water bed, swimming pool with diving board, and needs two drivers.*

#223

The first coin-operated video games appeared in the 1970s.

#224

Over a thousand years ago, monks in Europe invented the pretzel.

#225 *It was shaped like a child's arms crossed in prayer.*

#226

A **train** speeding around a curve doesn't fly off the tracks because the outside track is higher than the inside one.

#227

Solar cells

change sunlight to electricity.

#228

The electricity powers everything, from homes to satellites in space.

#229

Computer-printer ink is one of the most expensive liquids—it costs almost $5,000 a gallon.

#230

Since Benjamin Franklin invented swim flippers at age 11, kids have been coming up with some of the **coolest inventions**.

Here are a few:

#231

Swim flippers 1717
Benjamin Franklin, age 11

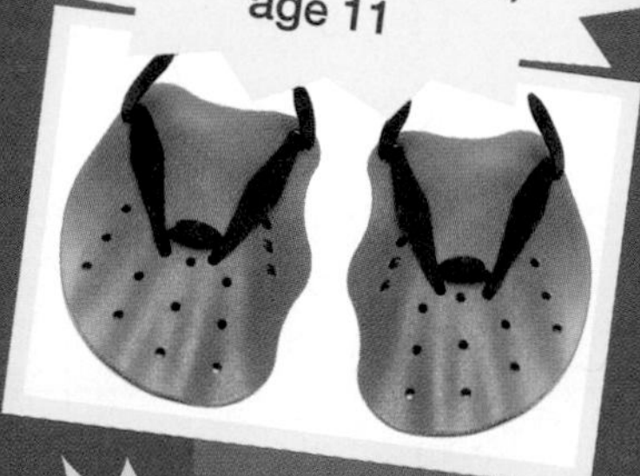

#232

Braille system for the blind 1824
Louis Braille, age 15

#233

Earmuffs 1873
Chester Greenwood age 15

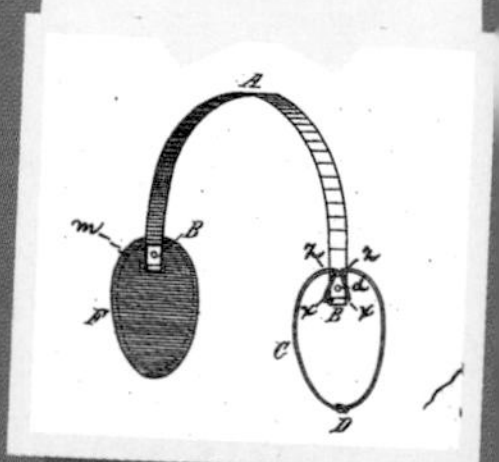

#234

Popsicle 1905
Frank Epperson, age 11

#235

Modern Christmas tree lights 1917
Albert Sadacca, age 15

#236

Snowmobile 1922
Joseph-Armand Bombardier, age 15

#237

Trampoline 1930
George Nissen, age 16

#238

Kiddie Stool 1987
Jeanie Low,
age 11

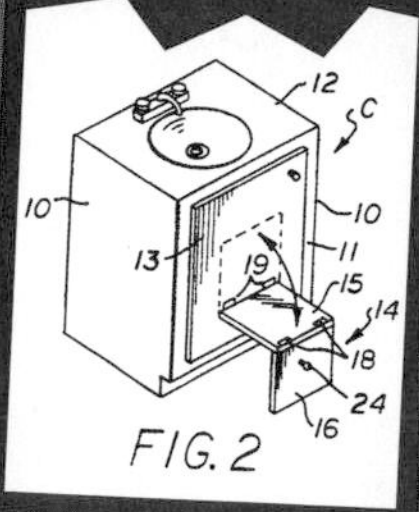

#239

Makin' Bacon
dish 1993
Abbey Fleck,
age 8

#240

No-spill pet
feeding bowl 1993
Alexia Abernathy,
age 11

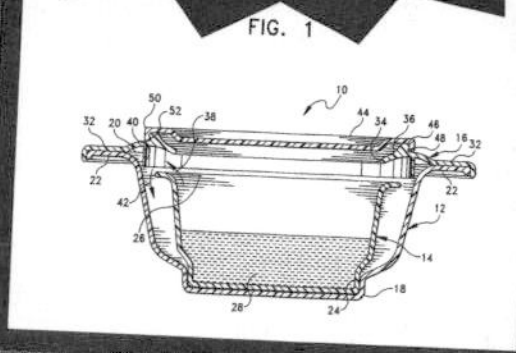

#241

Wristies 1994
Kathryn Gregory,
age 10

#242

Water Talkie 1997
Richie Stachowski,
age 11

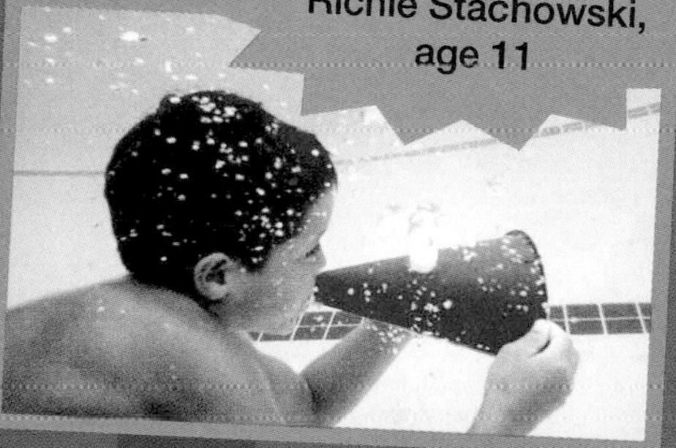

#243

Crayon holders 1999
Cassidy Goldstein,
age 11

#244

Magnetic locker
wallpaper 2006
Sarah Buckel,
age 14

#245

Cancer test 2012
Jake Andraka,
age 15

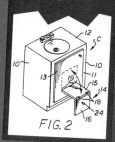

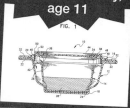

#246

Thomas Edison invented a **doll** with a built-in record player that could play one of a dozen nursery rhymes.

#247

Nearly every week a piece of **debris** from an old space mission falls to Earth.

#248

The epic 1977 movie *Star Wars* revolutionized **special effects** with its use of extended 3-D animation and perfection of the blue screen.

#249

All **broadcasting satellites** are in orbit 22,236 miles above Earth.

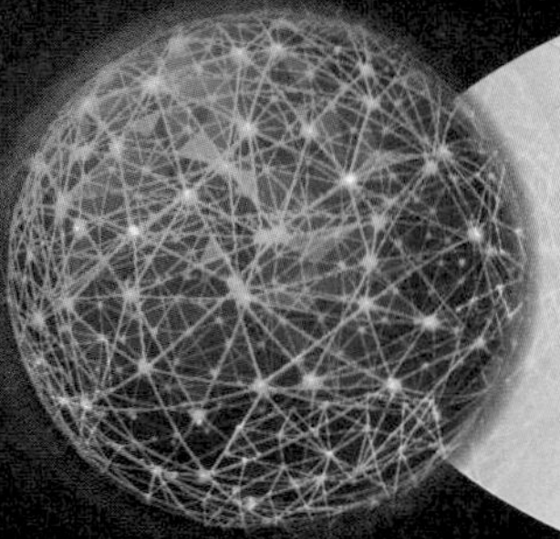

#250

The **Internet** was first called "Galactic Network."

#251

Astronauts become about 2 inches taller in the **zero gravity** of outer space.

#252

Without the pull of gravity, the spine grows longer.

#253

Roller coasters were invented back in 1884—and they still work the same way.

#254

The cars gain energy as they are pulled up to the highest peak. Then they use the energy to swoop up and down over the lower peaks, at speeds up to 150 miles per hour!

#255

Henn-na, a Japanese **hotel**, is the first hotel to be run by robots.

#256

A 12-foot-tall robot guards the entrance.

#257

A robot porter carries luggage and leads guests to their rooms.

#258 A small robot near the bed controls the lights and temperature.

#259 *It also answers questions about the time and weather.*

#260 A large, furry robot greets guests in Japanese and English.

#261 A dinosaur robot handles check-in.

#262

The first DIAL telephone, which made direct calls possible, was invented and built in 1889 by an undertaker, Almon B. Strowger.

#263

He invented it after the telephone operator kept putting callers through to her husband's undertaking business, instead of Strowger's.

#264

The first test of a package being delivered by a drone was on July 17, 2015.

Is my bedtime story ready yet, Mommy?
Just a few more minutes!

#265

The first humans wrote on clay tablets, which they baked to make into a hard surface.

#266

A jetpack is a powered backpack that lets a person fly.

#267

Astronauts wear jetpacks to move around in space outside their spacecraft.

I wish someone would invent a machine to do this!
4+6+
3+7+
5+4+

#268

Until 1935, dictionaries defined "computer" as "a person who works with numbers."

#269

An automatic **pasta-spinning fork** was invented in 1950.

#270

An ancient Greek man, Hero, invented the first coin-operated **vending machine**.

#271

He used it to sell holy water.

#272

Astronaut Scott Kelly set an American record in 2016 by spending nearly a year in **space**.

#273

The bird in the Twitter logo was originally named Larry.

Tweet!
Tweet!
Twit!
Larry, I've told you 140 times, it's tweet!

#274

The first vacuum cleaner, invented in 1901, was the size of a truck.

#275

It was hauled by horses and had a long hose to reach into houses.

#276

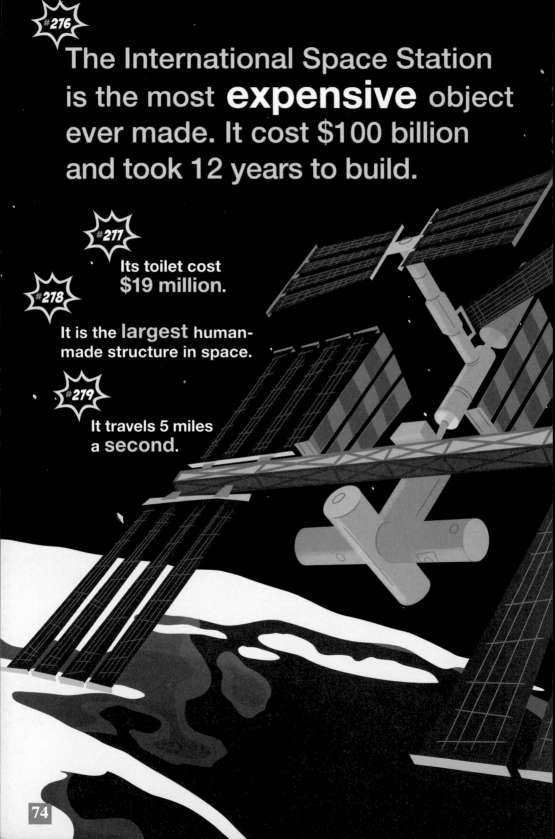

The International Space Station is the most **expensive** object ever made. It cost $100 billion and took 12 years to build.

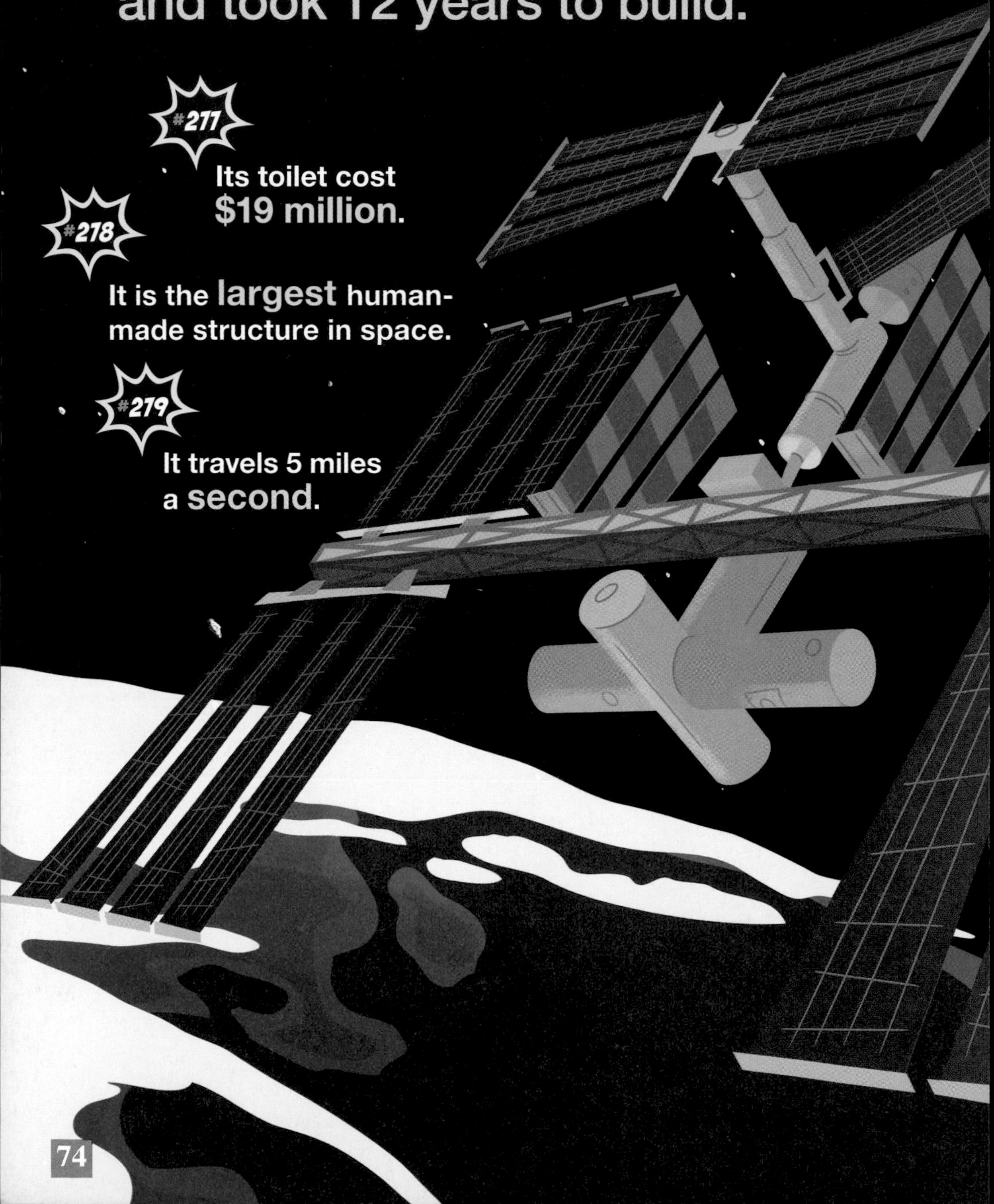

#277

Its toilet cost $19 million.

#278

It is the largest human-made structure in space.

#279

It travels 5 miles a second.

#281

Astronauts grow some foods from **seeds** inside.

#280

Astronauts sleep in **sleeping bags** attached to a wall, floor, or ceiling.

#282

Astronauts from **18** different countries have lived there.

#283

It can hold as many as six **astronauts**.

#284

It circles **Earth** more than 15 times a day at an altitude of 248 miles.

#285

It is as big as a five-bedroom **house**.

#286

It has a treatment plant that changes urine into **drinking water**.

#287

It is powered by an acre of **solar** panels.

#288

It passes 16 **sunrises** and **sunsets** every 24 hours.

#289 Some modern inventions come from ideas of the famous artist and inventor **Leonardo da Vinci**, who lived from 1452 to 1519!

#290 *Leonardo did not use these names, but each modern invention can be associated with a particular drawing from his notebooks and research.*

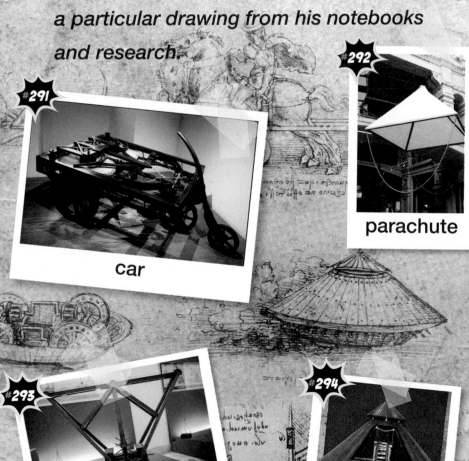

#291

car

#292

parachute

#293

crane

#294

tank

#295

steam engine

#296

airplane

#297

bicycle

#298

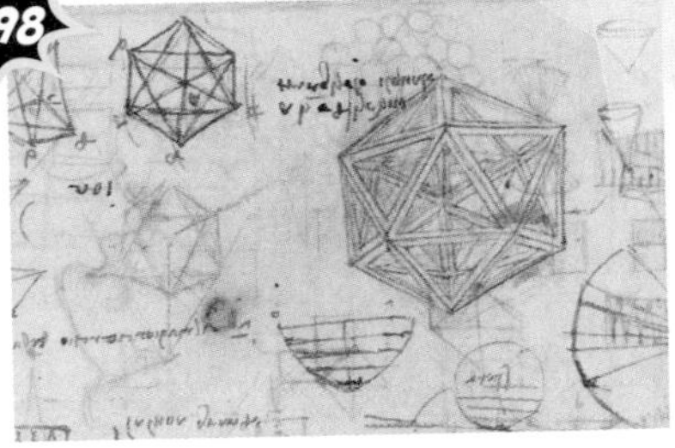

telescope

#299

helicopter

#300

swimming shoes

#301

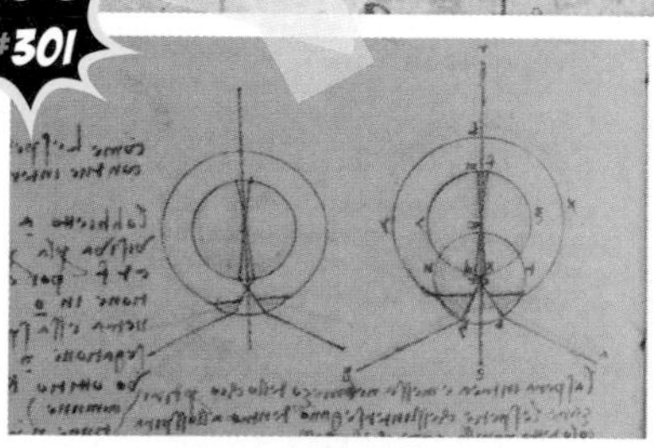

eyeglasses

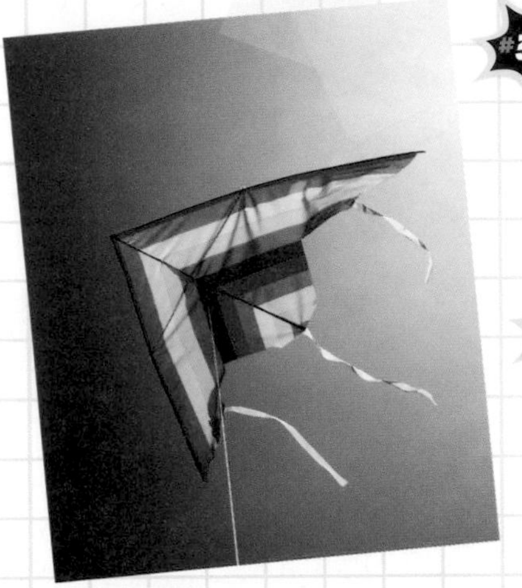

#302

The **kite** is the very first flying machine.

#303 *It is one of the oldest technological objects still in use.*

#304

It is believed that a Chinese cook invented **fireworks**, approximately 2,000 years ago.

Let's keep this between us.

#305

Jump jets rise straight up, like helicopters.

#306 *The jet engines point downward to lift off and backward to fly forward.*

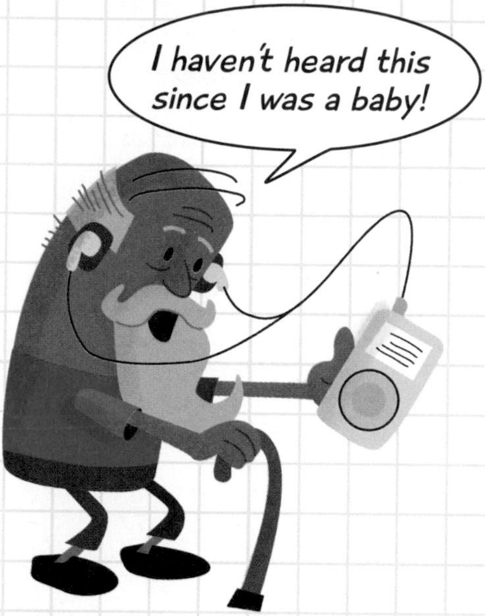

I haven't heard this since I was a baby!

#307

Some **iPods** can store 30,000 songs—enough to play a new one every day for almost 100 years.

#308

Ice cream

was invented in China.

#309

It was made of rice and milk packed in snow.

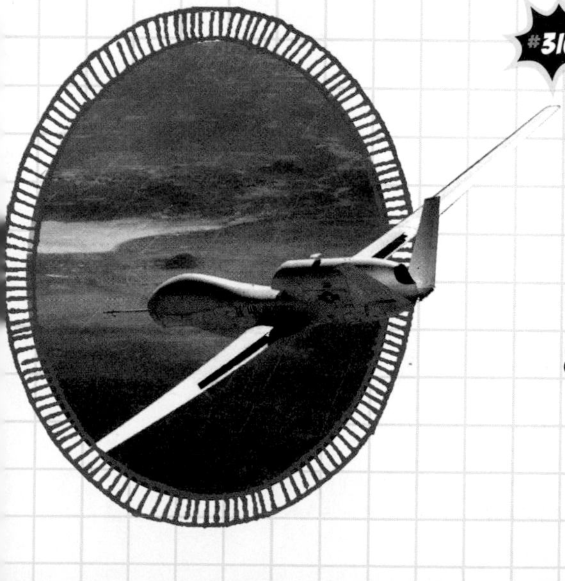

#310

The **Global Hawk** drone made the longest nonstop flight—8,600 miles—in 2001.

#311

People use UV (ultraviolet) pens to write invisible, secret messages.

[redacted] *The pen's UV light makes the message visible.*

[redacted]

ENIAC, introduced in 1946, was the first all-purpose, all-electronic computer.

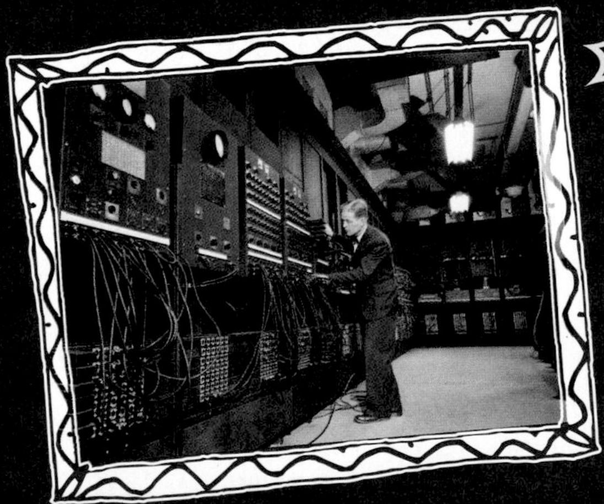

#314 *It was almost 9 feet tall, weighed 60,000 pounds, filled a large room, and could do 5,000 operations a second.*

#315

The **AS-2** drone record for longest time in the air is 81.5 hours (2015).

#316

When away from home, pet owners can use **Kittyo**, a computer app, to watch, speak to, and play with their cats.

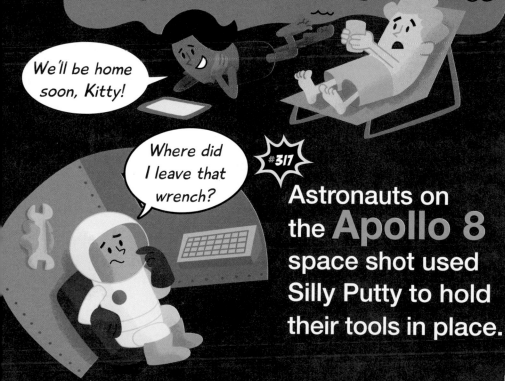

We'll be home soon, Kitty!

Where did I leave that wrench?

#317

Astronauts on the **Apollo 8** space shot used Silly Putty to hold their tools in place.

#318 Some of the world's top inventions sprang from *happy accidents!*

#319

Chef George Crum kept trying to make some fried potatoes crunchy enough for a very fussy customer—and invented **potato chips**, in 1853.

#320

John Pemberton was trying to develop a headache medicine when he stumbled on the formula for **Coca-Cola** in 1886.

#321

John Kellogg was looking for a bread substitute. He boiled some dough too long, baked it anyway—and invented **cornflakes** in 1898.

#322

Wilhelm Röntgen was sending electricity through a tube in 1895 when he accidentally found invisible rays shooting out—discovering **X-rays**.

#323

In 1907, when Leo Baekeland was trying to improve a varnish, he developed a light, strong material that could be shaped, inventing an early kind of **plastic**.

#324

In 1912, Harry Brearley was trying to find a metal that would not wear out—and invented **stainless steel.**

#325

In 1928, Dr. Alexander Fleming, while growing a dish of germs, noticed that a spot of green mold was killing them. That's how he discovered **penicillin**.

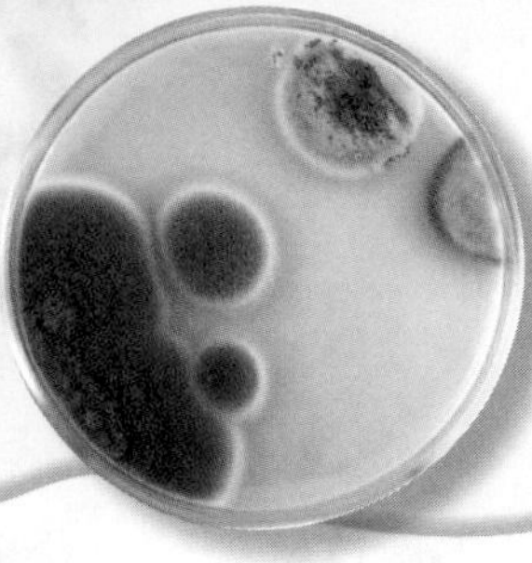

#326

Richard James invented the **Slinky** in 1943, after knocking a coil of wire off his desk and watching it fall step by step to the floor.

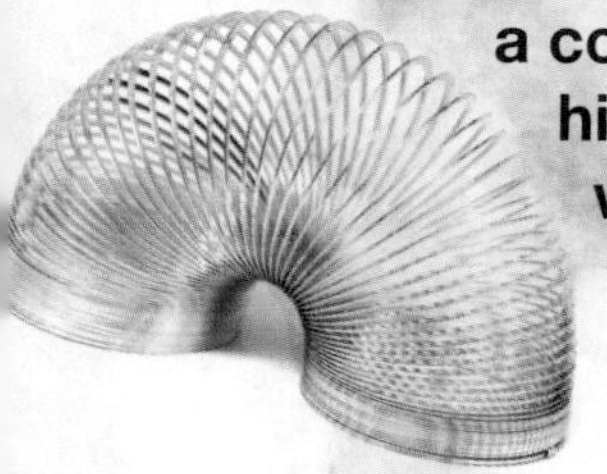

#327

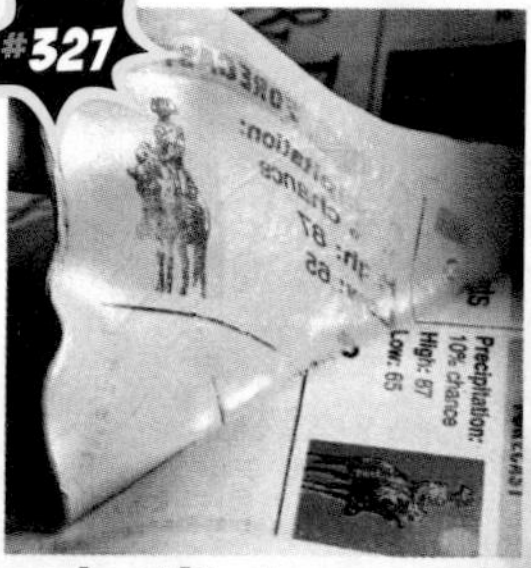

In 1943, during World War II, James Wright was looking for a rubber substitute—and created **Silly Putty**.

#328

The researcher Percy LeBaron Spencer walked by a radar tube in 1946 and noticed that a candy bar had melted in his pocket. It led him to invent the **microwave oven**.

#329

Joseph and Noah McVicker noticed that their product for cleaning wallpaper made a great art material—so they invented **Play-Doh** in 1956.

#330

George de Mestral was walking in the woods in 1948 and noticed burrs sticking to his clothes. That gave him the idea for **Velcro**.

#331

Harry Coover was testing clear plastics in 1951 and accidentally developed **Super Glue**—which stuck to everything.

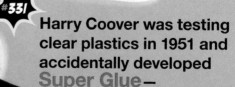

#332

A thin, see-through layer of **gold** covers the cockpit windows of some jet planes.

#333

Passing electricity through the gold melts ice on the window.

You should have gotten the gold windows.

#334

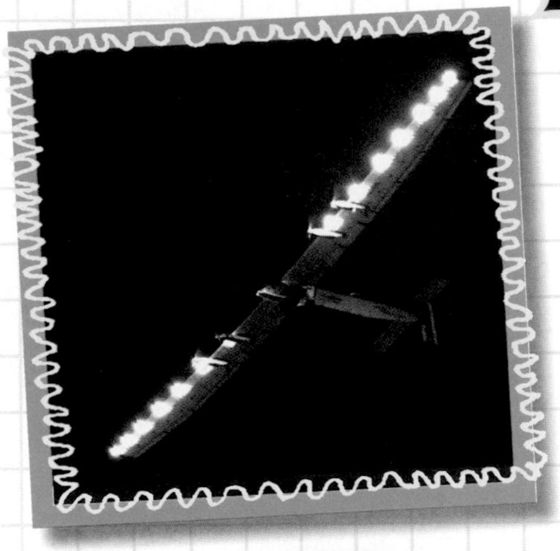

The **Solar Impulse 2** airplane was able to fly nonstop for 5 days in 2015, using solar cells by day and batteries at night.

I'm X's!

#335

The first 2-player **computer game** was an electronic version of tic-tac-toe.

#336

A spacecraft landed on a **comet** for the first time on August 6, 2014.

#337

The trip took 10 years and cost $1.5 billion!

#338

The first **telephone call** from New York to London in 1927 cost $25 a minute.

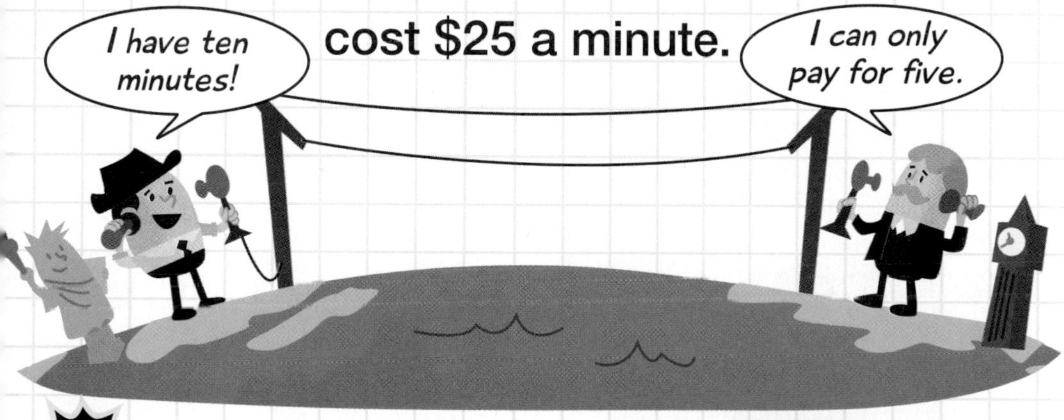

I have ten minutes!
I can only pay for five.

#339

The **laparoscope** is a medical tool that lets doctors use a tiny cut in the belly to insert a camera and see inside the body.

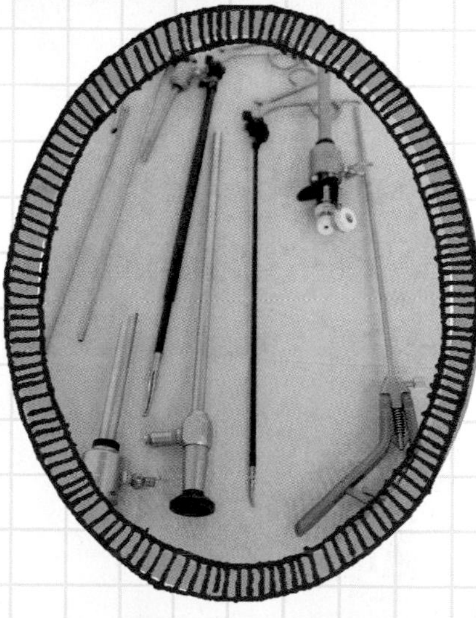

#340

Only **5 percent** of the world's population has ever been in an airplane.

#341

Salt and pepper for astronauts come in **liquid** form.

#342

If they were dry, the salt and pepper would float away.

#343

Early **bubble gum** was so sticky that popped bubbles had to be removed with turpentine.

#344

At 1,640 feet wide, the world's largest **radio telescope** in Pingtang County, China, is the size of 30 football fields.

#345

It searches the skies for signs of life and new galaxies.

#346

Until the discovery of rubber **erasers** in 1770, pencil marks were erased with lumps of fresh bread.

#347

The **cotton candy** machine was invented in 1897 by William Morrison, a dentist, and John Wharton, a candymaker.

#348

The first American invention **patent**, in 1790, was for soap.

#349

It's impossible to **whistle** in a space suit.

#350

There's not enough air inside the suit to make the sound.

#351

The lead in one **pencil** can draw a line 35 miles long.

#352

A **jumbo jet** holds enough fuel to drive an average car 4 times around planet Earth.

#353

It takes up to 80 percent less energy to make a ton of paper from **recycled paper** than from trees.

#354

Rockets must carry their own oxygen, since there is none in space.

#355

Drones, or UAVs (Unmanned Aerial Vehicles), are remote-controlled airplanes **without pilots** that vary from insect size to the size of jet planes—and can do many things.

#356

They deliver pizza and other packages.

#357

They track wildlife and combat poachers.

#358

They help farmers check crops and livestock.

#359

They carry medicines and supplies to dangerous places.

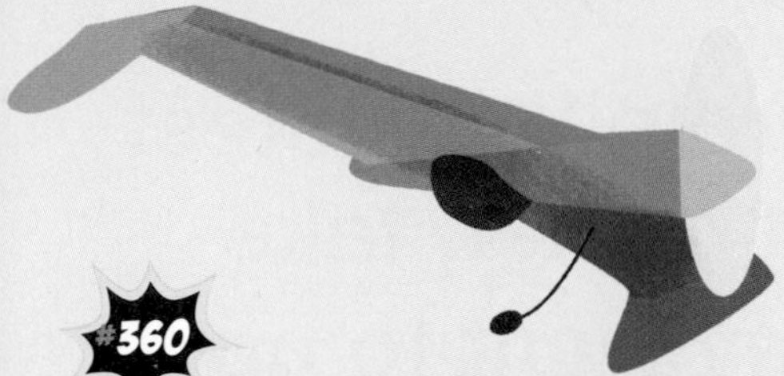

#360 They check weather and follow storms.

#361 They perform search-and-rescue missions after disasters.

#362 They help police find suspects.

#363 They monitor and put out forest fires.

#364 They film sports events.

#365

Super vehicles, from the fastest car to the fastest rocket, take people where they want to go in **record time!**

#366 Fastest gasoline-engine car: the **Hennessey Venom GT**, 2014—270.49 miles per hour

#367 Fastest speedboat: ***Spirit of Australia***, 1978—317.58 miles per hour

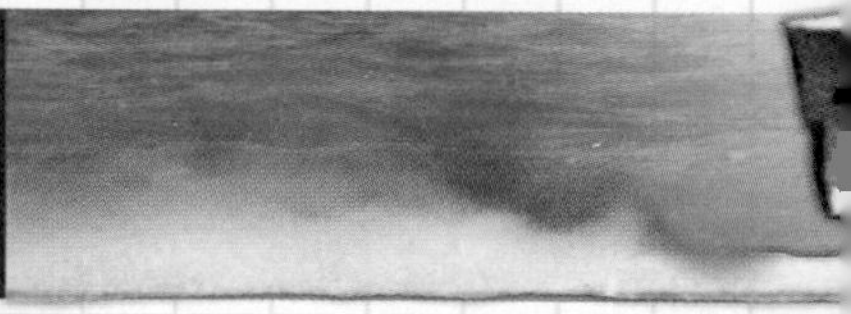

#368 Fastest train: Japan's **Maglev bullet train**, 2015—374.7 miles per hour

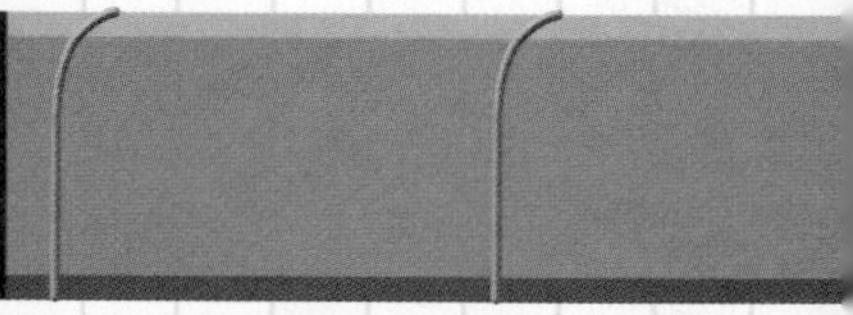

#369 Fastest motorcycle: **Ack Attack**, 2010—376.36 miles per hour

#370 Fastest jet-engine car: **Thrust SSC**, 1997—763.04 miles per hour

#371 Fastest airplane: **Lockheed SR 71 Blackbird**, 1976—2,193.6 miles per hour

#372 Fastest rocket: **New Horizons**, 2006—36,373 miles per hour

SPIRIT OF AUSTRALIA

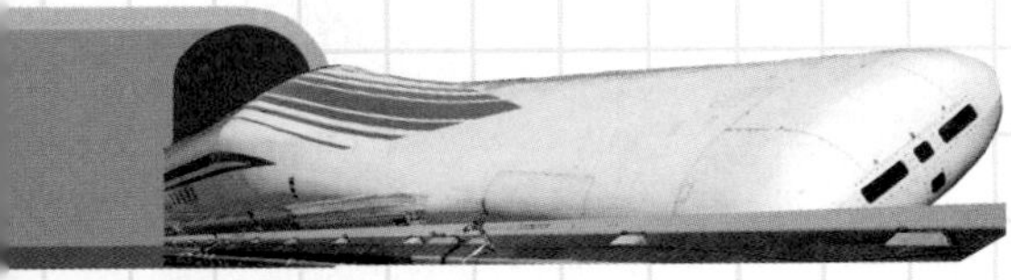

VARTA

Tivoli

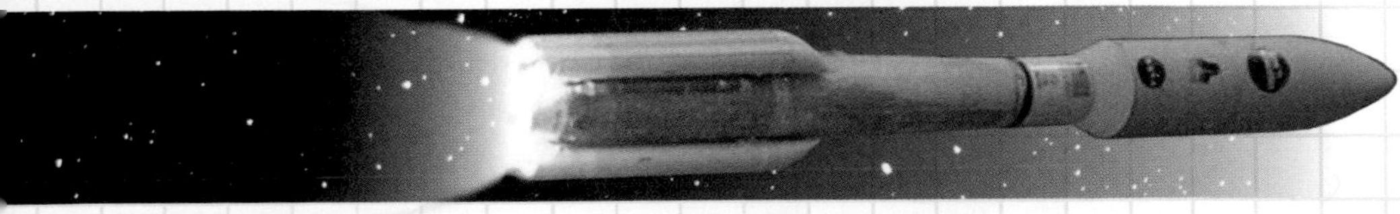

Index

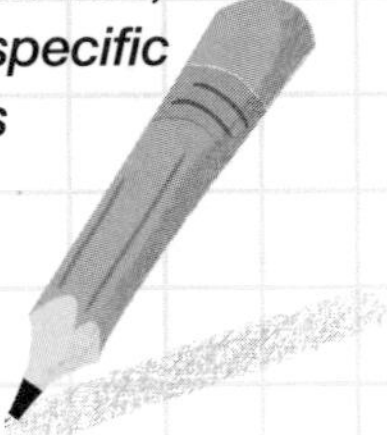
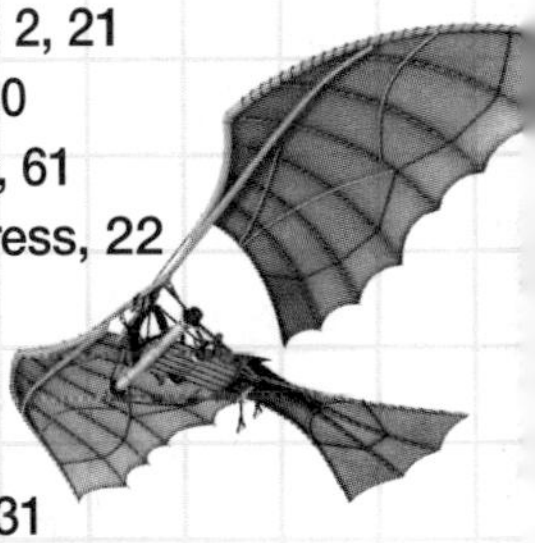

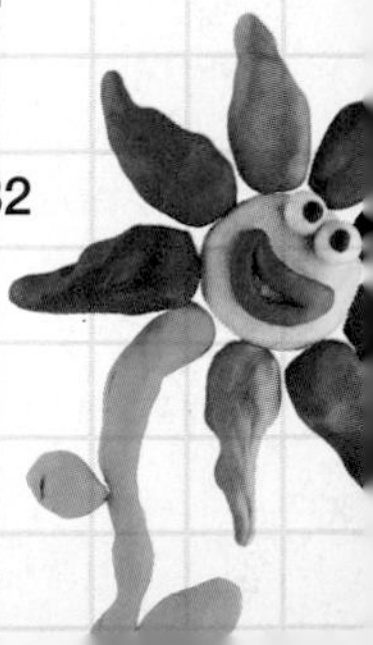